JUL 0 2 2013

19.95
J917.93

D1275613

NEVADA

Julie Murray

Big Buddy BOOKS
Explore the United States

VISIT US AT
www.abdopublishing.com

Published by ABDO Publishing Company, PO Box 398166, Minneapolis, MN 55439.

Copyright © 2013 by Abdo Consulting Group, Inc. International copyrights reserved in all countries. No part of this book may be reproduced in any form without written permission from the publisher. Big Buddy Books™ is a trademark and logo of ABDO Publishing Company.

Printed in the United States of America, North Mankato, Minnesota.
042012
092012

 PRINTED ON RECYCLED PAPER

Coordinating Series Editor: Rochelle Baltzer
Editor: Sarah Tieck
Contributing Editors: Megan M. Gunderson, BreAnn Rumsch, Marcia Zappa
Graphic Design: Adam Craven
Cover Photograph: *Shutterstock*: Andy Z.
Interior Photographs/Illustrations: *AP Photo*: Denis Beaumont (p. 23), Cal Sport Media via AP Images (p. 27), Michel Euler (p. 23), Julie Jacobson (p. 11), Jeff Klein (p. 25), North Wind Picture Archives via AP Images (p. 13); *Getty Images*: Tim Fitzharris/Minden Pictures (p. 30), Kean Collection (p. 27); *Glow Images*: © Imagebroker RM (p. 19), © Superstock (p. 9); *iStockphoto*: ©iStockphoto.com/andyb001 (p. 5), ©iStockphoto.com/Matt_Brown (p. 13), ©iStockphoto.com/coopermoisse (p. 21), ©iStockphoto.com/Janugio (p. 30), ©iStockphoto.com/natureniche (p. 30); *Shutterstock*: Bwilson (p. 19), Tina Darby (p. 29), Songquan Deng (p. 9), Amy Nichole Harris (p. 26), Philip Lange (p. 30), Dean Pennala (p. 30), perlphoto (p. 26), topseller (p. 11), Andy Z. (pp. 17, 27).

All population figures taken from the 2010 US census.

Library of Congress Cataloging-in-Publication Data

Murray, Julie, 1969-
  Nevada / Julie Murray.
    p. cm. -- (Explore the United States)
  ISBN 978-1-61783-366-3
  1. Nevada--Juvenile literature. I. Title.
  F841.3.M87 2013
  979.3--dc23
                    2012010552

Nevada

Contents

One Nation

The United States is a **diverse** country. It has farmland, cities, coasts, and mountains. Its people come from many different backgrounds. And, its history covers more than 200 years.

Today the country includes 50 states. Nevada is one of these states. Let's learn more about Nevada and its story!

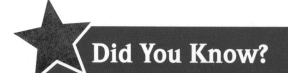

Did You Know?

Nevada became a state on October 31, 1864. It was the thirty-sixth state to join the nation.

Nevada's highest point is Boundary Peak. It is in the White Mountains on the state's western border.

5

NEVADA UP CLOSE

The United States has four main **regions**. Nevada is in the West.

Nevada has five states on its borders. Oregon and Idaho are north. Utah is east and Arizona is southeast. California is south and west.

Nevada has a total area of 110,572 square miles (286,380 sq km). About 2.7 million people live there.

REGIONS OF THE UNITED STATES

= West
= Midwest
= South
= Northeast

CANADA

WASHINGTON
MONTANA
NORTH DAKOTA
MINNESOTA
VERMONT
MAINE
NEW HAMPSHIRE
MASSACHUSETTS
OREGON
WISCONSIN
NEW YORK
IDAHO
SOUTH DAKOTA
MICHIGAN
RHODE ISLAND
CONNECTICUT
WYOMING
PENNSYLVANIA
IOWA
OHIO
NEW JERSEY
NEVADA
NEBRASKA
INDIANA
Washington DC ★
DELAWARE
ILLINOIS
WEST VIRGINIA
MARYLAND
PACIFIC OCEAN
UTAH
COLORADO
KANSAS
MISSOURI
VIRGINIA
CALIFORNIA
KENTUCKY
NORTH CAROLINA
ATLANTIC OCEAN
TENNESSEE
SOUTH CAROLINA
ARIZONA
OKLAHOMA
ARKANSAS
NEW MEXICO
MISSISSIPPI
GEORGIA
TEXAS
LOUISIANA
ALABAMA
FLORIDA
GULF OF MEXICO

ALASKA
MEXICO
HAWAII
PUERTO RICO

N
W E
S

7

IMPORTANT CITIES

Carson City is the **capital** of Nevada. The city is at the eastern base of the Sierra Nevada mountain range. Many of its buildings are from the 1800s, when it was a young mining town.

Las Vegas is the state's largest city, with 583,756 people. It is one of the most popular US vacation spots. The city is known for its hotels and **casinos**. Some of the hotels are among the world's largest.

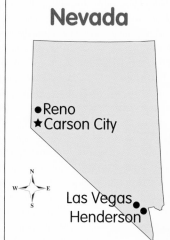

Nevada

●Reno
★Carson City

Las Vegas●
Henderson

There are many unusual landmarks in Las Vegas. People can visit copies of the Statue of Liberty (*above*) and the Eiffel Tower (*below left*)!

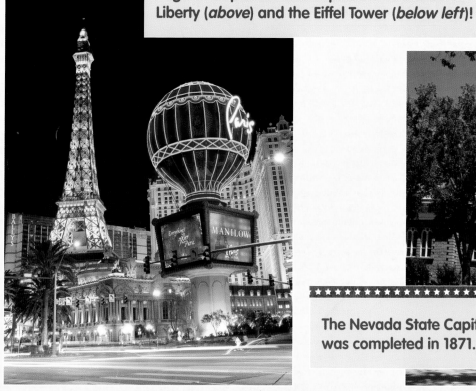

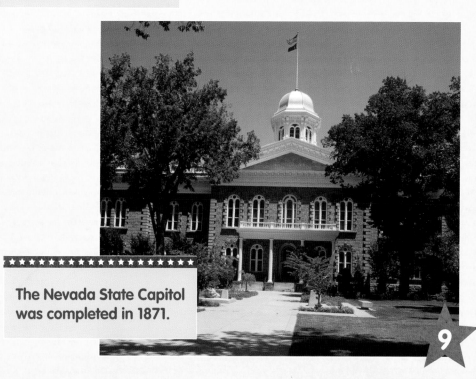

The Nevada State Capitol was completed in 1871.

Nevada's second-largest city is Henderson. It is home to 257,729 people. This fast-growing city is close to Las Vegas, Lake Mead, and the Hoover Dam.

Reno is the state's third-largest city, with 225,221 people. It is called "the Biggest Little City in the World." Like Las Vegas, Reno is known for its **casinos**.

The bright lights and hotels of Las Vegas can be seen from Henderson.

More than 100 hot air balloons fly in the Great Reno Balloon Race each year.

Nevada in History

Nevada's history includes Native Americans, explorers, and miners. Native Americans were the first people to live in what is now Nevada.

The first Europeans arrived in the 1770s. In 1843, explorer John C. Frémont visited the Sierra Nevadas and the Great **Basin**. Then, he reported what he saw.

In the 1800s, mines were built as silver and gold were found. As settlers arrived, the population grew. Nevada became a state in 1864.

Did You Know?

Today, Fremont Street in Las Vegas is named for John C. Frémont.

Native American petroglyphs (PEH-truh-glihfs) can be seen in Nevada. These drawings are thousands of years old. They tell stories from life at that time.

Frémont is remembered for exploring many parts of the western United States.

Timeline

1902

Gold was found in Goldfield. This brought many more miners to Nevada.

1864

Nevada became the thirty-sixth state on October 31.

1800s

Silver was found on Henry Comstock's land near Virginia City. This became known as the Comstock Lode.

1859

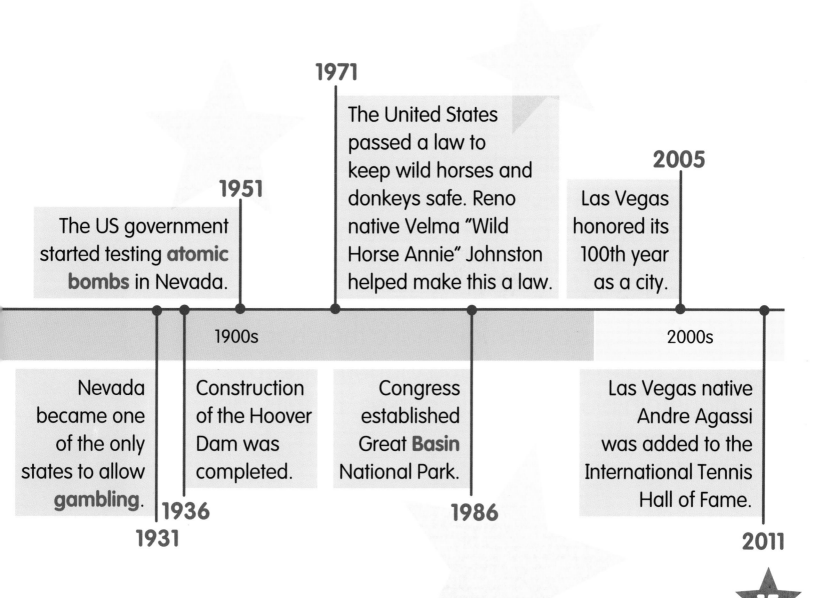

1971

The United States passed a law to keep wild horses and donkeys safe. Reno native Velma "Wild Horse Annie" Johnston helped make this a law.

2005

Las Vegas honored its 100th year as a city.

1951

The US government started testing **atomic bombs** in Nevada.

1900s

2000s

Nevada became one of the only states to allow **gambling**.

Construction of the Hoover Dam was completed.

Congress established Great **Basin** National Park.

Las Vegas native Andre Agassi was added to the International Tennis Hall of Fame.

1936

1931

1986

2011

Across the Land

Nevada has deserts, mountains, and lakes. The Great **Basin** covers central Nevada. The Sierra Nevadas are in the western part of the state. Parts of Lake Tahoe, Lake Mead, and the Colorado River are in Nevada.

Many types of animals make their homes in this state. These include bighorn sheep, mountain bluebirds, wild horses, rabbits, and rattlesnakes.

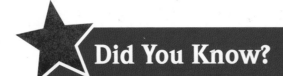

Did You Know?

In July, the average temperature in Nevada is 73°F (23°C). In January, it is 30°F (-1°C).

The Hoover Dam helps stop the Colorado River from flooding. It was built in 1936 and is still one of the largest US dams.

Earning a Living

Nevada is a popular vacation spot. Many people visit Las Vegas and the Hoover Dam. So, a lot of people in Nevada have jobs helping visitors. They may work at restaurants, at hotels, or as entertainers.

Other important businesses in Nevada include mining and manufacturing. And, many people work for the government. The state also has farms, including cattle farms.

Silver and gold are two important products mined in Nevada.

Hay grown in Nevada is shipped around the United States.

19

Natural Wonder

Valley of Fire State Park is Nevada's largest and oldest state park. It is in southeastern Nevada.

The park was named for its red sandstone formations. Over many years, wind, rain, and shifts in the earth cut the rock into unusual shapes. Today, people visit the park to hike, camp, and picnic.

Elephant Rock is a well-known rock formation in Valley of Fire State Park.

HOMETOWN HEROES

Many famous people have lived in Nevada. Andre Agassi was born in Las Vegas in 1970. He is a world-famous tennis player.

Agassi has won each of the world's four major tennis **tournaments**. These are the Australian Open, the French Open, Wimbledon, and the US Open. He also won a gold medal at the 1996 Summer Olympics.

Agassi won the French Open in 1999.

Agassi no longer plays in major tennis tournaments. Now, he only plays the sport for fun.

Wayne Newton was born in the state of Virginia in 1942. His real name is Carson Wayne Newton. In 1959, Newton got a job in Las Vegas. He sang and played instruments in a show at the Fremont Hotel and **Casino**. Over time, he became one of the city's biggest stars.

Some people call Newton "Mr. Las Vegas."

Tour Book

Do you want to go to Nevada? If you visit the state, here are some places to go and things to do!

 ## ⭐ Swim

Go for a dip in Lake Tahoe. This popular vacation spot is on the border between Nevada and California. People also boat, bike, hike, and ski in the area.

 ## ⭐ Discover

Visit Hoover Dam. You can cross the dam, which is 726 feet (221 m) high. Or, you can tour the inside of it!

 ## Cheer

See a Las Vegas sporting event, such as a rodeo. The city also hosts golf tournaments, auto races, and boxing matches.

 ## Remember

Learn about famous 1840s explorer Kit Carson in Carson City. Follow the Kit Carson Trail through town and see historic buildings.

 ## See

Walk down Las Vegas Boulevard. It is full of famous hotels, fun activities, and colored lights.

A GREAT STATE

The story of Nevada is important to the United States. The people and places that make up this state offer something special to the country. Together with all the states, Nevada helps make the United States great.

Did You Know?

Nevada gets less rain than any other state.

Lake Mead is a man-made lake near Las Vegas. People boat and swim there.

29

Fast Facts

Date of Statehood:
October 31, 1864

State Capital:
Carson City

Postal Abbreviation:
NV

Population (rank):
2,700,551
(35th most-populated state)

Flag:

Trees:
Single-leaf Piñon

Bristlecone Pine

Total Area (rank):
110,572 square miles
(7th largest state)

Flower: Sagebrush

Motto:
"All for Our Country"

Bird: Mountain Bluebird

Nickname:
Sagebrush State,
Silver State,
Battle Born State

Important Words

atomic bomb a bomb that uses the energy of atoms. Atoms are tiny particles that make up matter.

basin a large area of the ground that is lower than the land around it.

capital a city where government leaders meet.

casino a place where adults go to bet money on games.

diverse made up of things that are different from each other.

gambling betting money on games such as cards or slot machines.

region a large part of a country that is different from other parts.

tournament a set of games or matches held to find a first-place winner.

Web Sites

To learn more about Nevada, visit ABDO Publishing Company online. Web sites about Nevada are featured on our Book Links page. These links are routinely monitored and updated to provide the most current information available.

www.abdopublishing.com

Index